# Empire of Shadows
# Hugh McFadden

**salmon**poetry

Published in 2012 by
Salmon Poetry
Cliffs of Moher, County Clare, Ireland
Website: www.salmonpoetry.com
Email: info@salmonpoetry.com

Copyright © Hugh McFadden, 2012

ISBN 978-1-908836-13-7

All rights reserved. No part of this publication may be reproduced or transmitted in any form or by any means, electronic or mechanical, including photography, recording, or any information storage or retrieval system, without permission in writing from the publisher. The book is sold subject to the condition that it shall not, by way of trade or otherwise, be lent, resold or otherwise circulated without the publisher's prior consent in any form of binding or cover other than that in which it is published and without a similar condition, including this condition, being imposed on the subsequent purchaser.

COVER ARTWORK: © *Luba V Nel* | *Dreamstime.com*
COVER DESIGN: *Siobhán Hutson*

*Salmon Poetry receives financial support from The Arts Council*

## Shadow & Substance

'For, tell me, do you think our prisoners could see anything of themselves or their fellows except the shadows thrown by the fire on the wall of the cave opposite them?

– Plato, *The Republic*, Bk. VII, S. VII, 515
(*The Simile of the Cave*)

## Inferno

'O frati,' dissi, 'che per cento milia
perigli siete giunti a l'occidente …

'O brothers!' I began, 'woe to the west
Through perils without number now have we reach'd …'

– Dante, *Inferno*, Canto XXVI, 112-114

## The End of All

The end of all is death, and man's life passeth away suddenly as a shadow.

– Thomas a Kempis, *The Imitation of Christ*, Bk 1, Chap. XXIII

## Atomic Age

'We, who live in what we ourselves have called the Atomic Age, have acquired a peculiar facility for standing back and reflecting on our own history as if it were a phenomenon that took place five thousand years ago. We like to talk about our time as if we had no part in it. We view it as objectively as if it existed outside ourselves, in a glass case. If you are looking for the Atomic Age, look inside yourself: because you are it. And so, alas, am I.'

– Thomas Merton, *The Ascent to Truth*, 5

# Acknowledgements

Acknowledgements are due to the editors of the following magazines, journals and e-zines in which some of these poems appeared:

*Arabesque* (Algeria); *The Burning Bush 2* (Issue 4, 2012); *Census: The Second Seven Towers Anthology*; *Cyphers*; *Hartnett Echoing – Poems in Celebration of Michael Hartnett* (Revival Press/Limerick Writers' Centre, 2012); *The Irish Catullus*: or One Gentleman of Verona (ed. Ronan Sheehan); *The Irish Times*; *Light Years* (A Broadsheet for Pearse Hutchinson at 80); *The Poetry Bus*; *Poetry Ireland Newsletter*; *Poetry Ireland Review*; *poetsagainstwar/uk*; *poetsagainstthewar.org* (USA); *The Red Wheelbarrow* (St. Andrews); *Revival* (Limerick); *Shine On Anthology* (Dedalus Press); *Southword* (Cork); *The Stony Thursday Book* (Limerick), *Windows Poetry Anthology 2012* (eds Heather Brett and Noel Monaghan).

# Contents

PREFACE: Carmina 1 / Carmen 1: The Dedication     13

| | |
|---|---|
| Below the Bridge | 15 |
| Posthumous Letter To An Old Friend | 16 |
| Even the birds are still … | 17 |
| Five Zen Masters | 18 |
| Move Over Mr L | 19 |
| Lennon's 'God' Song Remixed | 20 |
| Late News Just In | 22 |
| Ineluctable Modalities | 23 |
| Post-Shematic Stress | 24 |
| Riposte to Shem | 24 |
| Poldy Lives! | 24 |
| Transfixed by McNeil's Nebula in Orion | 25 |
| New Blossom Therapy | 26 |
| Mise en scène on the Street | 27 |
| Nelson in the Doldrums | 31 |
| Pressman takes his ease | 32 |
| Assisi: At the great basilica | 33 |
| Reflections in Café Rio, Dublin | 34 |
| Blues in the Afternoon | 35 |
| Sporting Life Blues | 36 |
| Adiós to George W. Bush | 37 |
| Late Apocalypse | 38 |
| Shadow & Substance | 39 |
| Above the Underground | 40 |
| Collateral Damage | 41 |
| Tokyo Pictures | 42 |
| Bright morning, startling light | 43 |
| Splitting the Light | 44 |
| Hiroshima Fragment | 45 |
| The Temperature Was X Degrees | 46 |
| Falling 'Fat Man' Blues | 47 |
| Empire of Shadows | 49 |
| Light and Shadow | 50 |
| Fire as Trophy | 51 |

| | |
|---|---|
| Roadmaps and Roadmaps: the Attraction of Opposites | 52 |
| Lebanon, July 2006: The U.N. Security Council Meets | 53 |
| Lost in Samarra: One G.I. | 54 |
| Blind Faith | 55 |
| Moon shots and other shots | 56 |
| Pick a Bale of Cotton | 57 |
| Shadow Land | 58 |
| Chasing the Wind | 59 |
| In the midst of life … | 60 |
| Getting One's Teeth Into Time | 61 |
| Written with a thin black pen | 62 |
| Quite Early One Morning | 63 |
| Title Not Needed | 64 |
| Sound Hieroglyphs in the Eye & Ear | 65 |
| David's Farewell | 67 |
| Nine Mays Later | 69 |
| Good Vibes | 71 |
| Encountering the poet | 72 |
| The Season Turns | 73 |
| End of July | 74 |
| Local Nightlight | 75 |
| So slow, adagio | 76 |
| Gathering Rosebuds | 77 |
| Nov. 2008, Dawson Street, Dublin | 78 |
| The Cold at the Top of the World | 79 |
| By the Pool of Despond | 80 |
| Early Flashback | 81 |
| The Falcarragh Blues | 82 |
| Survival of the oddest | 83 |
| Christmas 2010 | 84 |
| Far Behind the Snow | 85 |
| Code Name 'Geronimo' | 86 |
| Digital Bytes …The | 87 |
| Movable Type | 88 |
| Almost Noon in Dallas | 89 |

*About the Author*   91

# Carmina 1
### *(Gaius Valerius Catullus)*

Cui dono lepidum novum libellum
arida  modo pumice expolitum?
Corneli, tibi: namque tu solebas
meas esse aliquid putare nugas;
iam tum, cum ausus es unus Italorum
omne aevum tribus explicare cartis ...
doctis, Iuppiter, et laborioris!
Quare habe tibi quidquid hoc libelli –
qualecumque, quod, o patrona virgo,
plus uno maneat perenne saeclo!


# Carmen 1: The Dedication
### *(after Catullus)*

To whom shall I present this dainty new book
freshly polished up and smoothed with parched pumice?
To you, Cornelius: for you always noticed
my fragmentary trifles were still worthwhile;
back then, when you alone among Italians
dared to explicate the whole world's history
in three volumes – well-versed and hard-wrought, by Jove!
So here it is, this little book: take and keep
it, such as it is, for all that it is worth;
and, O Muse, may it live for more than an Age.

# Below the Bridge

The sun had warmed the wooden seat for me
on the bank of the River Fane
situated below the old stone bridge
at Inniskeen. And as I write this verse
out, Patrick Kavanagh, I think of you
sitting below the bridge at Baggot Street
on the bank of the Grand Canal,
one warm and sunny summer's day
sometime in the middle 'Sixties –
perhaps the year was Sixty-Four or Six –
Anyway, you sat there then, as tranquil
as any Buddha ever did,
although, of course, you said yourself
you messaged no message at all
only simple joy at nature's beauty
and, by God's grace, peace at its heart.

As I write this, the sound of the water,
while it rushes over the flashing stones
rippling and breaking in the clear daylight,
mingles with the strains of music
drifting on the air near your own Centre,
as a white butterfly flits by the brown
river – its lush green bank all overgrown –
My heart's spirit lifts with the rising day:
All the cares of the city far away.

# Posthumous Letter To An Old Friend

*(i.m. Pat Paul McGowan, d. 13/12/2003)*

Pat,
Grief, like death, is so personal.
How could you go without saying goodbye?
Slipping the coil from here to eternity.

"What is the use of talking
And there is no end of talking
No end of things in the heart."

And, now, only silence:
Is there an end to silence?

Today I searched in Grafton Street
for the site of the Eblana bookstore
beside the Kum Tong restaurant:
How many hours did we spend there
talking, talking the alphabet …
only very, very, late at night now
is it a quiet street where old ghosts meet
talking, talking the alphabet …

words
words are all I've got
with which to say goodbye.

Liked the songs at the funeral
though, especially Dylan's
*Tomorrow is a Long Time* –
"If today was not an endless highway" –

and *Retro Me*, Michael Hartnett.

Goodbye old friend
old soul buddy:
Put a word in for me,
if you can, over there
on the other side.

# Even the birds are still ...

Overcast afternoon in February
the cherry tree in my back garden
is leafless, the outline of its bare branches
cupped upwards, classic candelabra,
its lines as clean and clear as any drawing:
and sitting in it are five birds still
and quiet as Buddhist monks meditating.

But this garden is not really mine at all,
although it's registered in my name:
I'm just the latest temporal caretaker.
The real owner also owns the Buddhist birds
and He doesn't need to prove His deed of title.

# Five Zen Masters

Five blackbirds sit still
meditating in the snow:
black, white & yellow.

# Move Over Mr L

Whatever gets ya thru' the night
it's all right, it's all right –
as long as you don't abuse it,
yourself or someone else –
it's all right, it's all right
(hold me, darlin', etcetera).

Whatever gets ya thru' the night
it's all right, it's all right –
as long as you don't hurt yourself
with too much dope or booze –
it's all right, it's all right, –
and as long as you realise
that God cannot be mocked –
it's all right, it's all right.

Whatever gets ya thru' the night
it's all right, it's all right
(etcetera, etcetera).

# Lennon's 'God' Song Remixed

Lennon's a concept
by which we can measure
our pain:
I'll say it again,
Lennon's a concept
by which we can measure
our pain.

I don't believe in magic,
I don't believe in I-ching,
I do believe in bible,
I don't believe in tarot,
I don't believe in Hitler,
I do believe in Jesus,
I don't believe in Kennedy,
I don't believe in Buddha,
I don't believe in mantra,
I don't believe in Gita,
I don't believe in yoga,
I don't believe in kings,
I don't believe in Elvis,
I don't believe in Zimmerman,
I don't believe in Beatles,
I just believe in me,
Jesus and me,
and that's reality.

The dream's not over,
that's what I say:
The dream's not over.
Yesterday
he was dreamweaver,
now he's dead John,
he was the walrus,
but now he's gone.

And so dear friends,
you just have to carry on:
The dream's not over –

his dream is over

# Late News Just In

James Joyce is dead.

He died of a Monday
at 2.15 a.m.
in the morning,
January 13th
1941, a
very long time ago.

Sometimes it takes a long
time for news to break through
to this ire land.

James Joyce is dead.

He died of an ulcer
acute duodiddlum
brought on by far too much
drinkum, his 'white lightning'
diddled him in the end,
jejunum it did him:
his body writhing like
a fish, in agony.

Switch on the lights:
James Joyce is dead –
he's buried in Zurich.

What's the story?
That's the story.
End of story.

# Ineluctable Modalities

Poor Lucia Joyce, lost in her own dance,
the light of her name quenched by a dark
alcoholic gene; seed of her befuddled granddad,
the gene that drove her dad to babble
his Nighttown nightmare, his Finnegans Wake.

Poor Lucia Joyce; the pool she drowned in
was her father's pool.

## Post-Shematic Stress

James Joyce got langers on language –
and Beckett woke up in the horrors.


## Riposte to Shem

It was at Kinsale, not Baginbun,
that Ireland's cause was lost and won.


## Poldy Lives!

'Bloom is a cod'

graffito seen
on Dame Street wall
in Dublin on
Bloomsday,
2004.

# Transfixed by McNeil's Nebula in Orion

It lies at the edge of the universe
nestling behind a cluster of galaxies
just 12 billion light years away from us
a mysterious arc of brilliant red light
in a swirling cocoon of red-hot gas
containing about a million bluish stars –
it's called the Lynx Arc Stellar Nursery.

Behind it, the Messier Seventy-Eight
gas cloud pulses with indescribable
energy. Slowly, slowly, after all these
years, a star embedded in its placental
nebula emerges to us. A star is born.

# New Blossom Therapy

My heart jumps again
with the shock recognition
of budding growth, the first spring
moment of the year – 2006:
this time it's the tree
seen from a bedroom window,
a copper beech, its snowy
mantilla of tiny buds
on its head, proud as a bride
dressed to meet her groom
this soul who survived winter.

## Mise en scène on the Street
*(i.m. Ronnie Drew)*

When Sackville Street
was ransacked by
local scumbags
or gurriers –
(native villains
red white and blue
Jackeens, untrue Dubs) –
who stuffed their sacks
and bags with loot
and scarpered down
O'Connell Street ...

Where Big Jim Larkin –
fiery agitator,
would-be liberator
(after the great-cloaked Dan
with his wounded angels) –
raised aloft his arms
in supplication ...

*get up off your knees*
*stand on your own feet*

And the long-lost Chief,
Charles Stewart Parnell,
at the Rotunda,
pointing his finger
at the hospital
where the women lie-in ...

*no man has the right*
*to fix the boundary*
*of a nation*

Near this same scene,
within gunshot,
stood Pádraig Pearse
reading aloud
the Proclamation
(at the very spot
where all the postmen
filled their bulging sacks)
proudly intoning
those famous words ...

*Irishmen and
Irishwomen:
In the name of God
and of the dead...*

Where James Connolly
marched to the GPO
from Liberty Hall
and raised the Starry Plough ...

*The worker is the slave
of the capitalist
society, the
female worker is
the slave of that slave*

Only a stone's throw
away in space-time
WB Yeats
stood and declared:

*you have disgraced
yourselves again*

And, again in
Sixty-six, shots
rang out sharply on

rooftops once looked down
on by stony-faced
Admiral Nelson

(*it's not beautiful,*
said Senator Yeats,
*grey brick upon brick,*
wrote Louis McNeice) ...

Nelson's Pillar –
rude reminder
of the power
of an empire,
its former glory,
and Horatio
Nelson's victory
at Trafalgar ...

*kiss me, Hardy*

Nelson's Pillar –
Joyce's omphalos

phallic standing stone,
a naval navel,
Anna Livia's
tight belly-button
right in the centre
of the hunting ground –
pricking a summit,
a peak on a plinth,
a towering spire
piercing the lowering
Hibernian womb ...

*ripe pears, apples and
juicy oranges*

Round the corner
stood Jasser Joyce,
leaning on his stick
at the heart of his
own metropolis,
paring his nails
while the ould wans,
all the shawlies,
hawked their fruity wares

*apples and oranges
and ripe juicy pears*

Then *The Dubliners*,
in their effrontery
and high drollery,
sang out their ballad:

*But one-thirty in
the morning, without
a bit of warning,
Nelson took a powdher
and he blew: oh poor
old Admiral Nelson
toora-loo*

They're nearly all
gone, now, to their
eternal rest.

# Nelson in the Doldrums

The lair, the lying place, is An Lár
where upright Nelson was exploded
into a stone stump, into rubble.

The one-eyed adulterer's head
stares blankly at the curious visitor
wandering around the museum's centre ...

now, warning lights blink on the Spire
while ageing Dubs dream of the Pillar.

# Pressman takes his ease
*(For John Banville)*

Sometimes, in these latter days of chaos,
for me,
love
is making a conscious decision not to play
again the heavy metal of that old hard news:

the days of hot metal are with De Valera –
cold, as buried bones, in his iconoclastic grave.

# Assisi: At the great basilica

In a sacred place
in a sacred zone
at the mid-day hour
on the mountaintop
seated in the piazza
of San Francesco,
carrying bread and water:
the basilica's stone wall
supports me in the noon heat
as I sit and wait,
patiently as possible,
during the long Holy Hour.

The heat continues to rise
a time for meditation:
in front of me a fountain.

# Reflections in Café Rio, Dublin

The dimensions differ
one from another:
but, in truth, we all
live in a box of air.

Sometimes,
when the sun shines,
we're taken for a stroll
in the freedom of light:
We are all on leave
in each day's sunlight

Yes, Jordan got it right
a long, long, time ago.

23rd September, 2005
The Feast Day of St. Pio

# Blues in the Afternoon
*(i.m. Shay McGonagle)*

Dear Shay,
My good friend John Jordan used to say:
'some of my best friends are dead'.
I know now how he felt then.

You left us without saying goodbye:
and, after so many years in show
business, as you called it,
no obituary was written
and no news item marked your passing –
not even a line drawing.

Do you remember (of course you do)
that old Woody Guthrie song
'So long, it's been good to know you',
well, that was more or less how I felt –

that, and the feeling you used to get
when a bluesman with soul sang the blues,
Sonny Terry and Brownie McGhee
say, on this *Sporting Life Blues*.

Wish I could sing it for you:
but, where you have gone, you don't need it.

'So long, it's been good to know yuh
So long, it's been good to know yuh
So long, it's been good to know yuh,
This dusty old dust's getting' mah home
And I've got to be driftin' along.

# Sporting Life Blues

Most of my best friends are dead
and gone: most were alcoholic
and died early. I miss them ...
Michael and Shay, Pat and John and
all the others, known and unknown
by their first and Christian names ...

We are such stuff as alcohol kills.

Yes, alcohol's a cunning beast.

May the good Lord quench our thirst
in the beauty of His creation:
may we learn to walk the walk
on the road to our destination.

# Adiós to George W. Bush

Goodbye, George Dubya, adiós amigo:
Ya know, we're really gonna miss the way
you slaughtered all those pesky foreigners,
ya know, those Eyeracki guys from Eyerack
Eyeran, and that other strange place, Afghan,
or whatever those weird Muslims call it.

Yeah, we're really gonna miss the great way
you slaughtered the ol' English language:
And aren't you the guy who said so clearly:
"I just want you to know that when we talk
about war, we're really talking about peace."
Wow, George Orwell would have loved that.

So, let me shake the hand of the man who said:
"I'm honored to shake the hand of a brave Iraqi
who had his hand cut off by Saddam Hussein."
Yeah, we sure did misunderestimate you.

## Late Apocalypse

The patient may be awake or dreaming:
he seems to be looking out over roofs
ablaze with lights, or is it a firestorm?
It is night, but what should be dark is lit
repeatedly by bursts of fire or light.

The cityscape turns into a seascape.
In turn, the sea turns into a desert,
where a storm whips up the sand of the sea:
the sand is running high in waves of blood,
the sky or the sea is a storm of fire.

Is this the start of the Apocalypse?
Is this a vision of past or future?

The door to the patient's room is locked.
The walls are so thick that no sound escapes.

# Shadow & Substance

All the shadows on the wall of the cave
are forms, shades of the imagination:
but the fire's real enough – elemental
simile for our alienation
from reality, mankind's passion
to escape into dreams of illusion.

It is easier to look at shadows,
or reflections of things in water,
than at the fire consuming real matter.

# Above the Underground

They came in the afternoon
on the first day that London
was ringed and stabbed by fire:
shortly after the sirens wailed
a swarm of droning planes
appeared in the city sky –
over 300 bombers
and 600 fighter planes.

Most of them came after dark:
their incendiaries falling
amid the thump and crash
of the anti-aircraft guns –
fires consumed the city centre,
flames crackling, firemen calling.

For 57 days and nights
the Blitz raged through the shaken city.
Then, as suddenly as they came,
they were gone: the planes flew east –
the sky at night strangely silent,
save for the odd false alarm,
the eerie wail of a siren …

*Dead leaves still rattled on like tin …*

Now and then a siren wailed.

*Shadows rising on you and me;*
*Shadows rising on you and me …*

And on the 20,000 dead.

# Collateral Damage

It was Jacques de Lacretelle
who said: "The city has a face,
the country has a soul."

And wasn't it Bomber Harris –
of Bomber Command fame –
who said that Würtsburg was
"a burnable city....",
that is should burn quite well?

And where, now, are the souls
of the city of Würtsburg?
Where the souls of all
the eager bombers?

# Tokyo Pictures

You can see the picture if you want to —
charred remains of Japanese civilians
after the firebombing of Tokyo —
but it's more real if you imagine it:

*Imagine.*

The key development for the bombing of Japan was the B-29, which had an operational range of 3,250 nautical miles (6,019 km); almost 90% of the bombs dropped on the home islands of Japan were delivered by this type of bomber:

*Imagine.*

# Bright morning, startling light

Awakening to a clear blue sky
cherry blossom cluster swaying
in a light breeze on a May morning.
A plane drones over at a height
and the thought flashes into my mind:
Hiroshima – Nagasaki – light
exploding in a vast surge of fire.

# Splitting the Light

The Age of Reason ushered in
this time, this Age of Anxiety,
produced the atomic shadow.

The scientists have split the light:
but they can't illuminate the shadow.

Splitting the atom was the easy part:
enlightening the shade's more recondite.

We live in a time of startling shadow.

# Hiroshima Fragment

The shadows on the wall
of our atomic age
are sacred: they reflect
the irradiated
light
that we have fractured.

# The Temperature Was X Degrees

*(i.m. The Unknown Shadow)*

The *Enola Gay* pilot sits wrapped
in his fur-lined leather jacket
to keep out the cold of upper space:
his co-pilot reads the zoned map
of the city doomed to be consumed
in the inferno of blinding light

the plane breathes out a plume of fumes.

Soundless, the 'Little Boy' device falls
in slow motion, receding in space
and, like a star, it implodes-explodes

far below, the atomic base surges.


II

Paul W. Tibbets was no Dante:
the shades he left behind were shadows
of human persons, stamped on stone steps.

# Falling 'Fat Man' Blues

As,

*Falling leaf and fading tree...*

'Bock's Car' took off from Tinian
Island in the Marianas...

*Lines of white in a sullen sea...*

carrying the 'Fat Man' bomb
heading for Kokura city ...

*Shadows rising on you and me;*
*Shadows rising on you and me.*

Few things went according to plan ...
*Goodbye Summer! Goodbye! Goodbye!...*
St. Elmo's Fire danced on the plane ...
*Goodbye Summer! Goodbye! Goodbye!*

The target was obscured by haze ...
*Hush! a voice from the far away!*
*'Listen and learn', it seems to say,*
*'All the tomorrows shall be as today.*
*All the tomorrows shall be as today'.*

An aircraft crewman, Jacob Baser,
said there was no sense taking it home,
the 'Fat Man', as they called the bomb ...
*The cord is frayed, the cruse is dry,*
*The link must break, and the lamp must die –*

Nagasaki now the target:
the die was cast, the fate was set ...

*Goodbye to Hope! Goodbye! Goodbye!*
*Goodbye to Hope! Goodbye! Goodbye! ...*

At 11.02 the 'Fat Man'
began to fall towards the city ...
*What are we waiting for? Oh, my heart!*
*What are we waiting for, you and I?*

At altitude it exploded
over Nagasaki city ...
*A pleading look, a stifled cry.*

*Goodbye, forever!*
*Goodbye, forever!*
*Goodbye! Goodbye! Goodbye!*

# Empire of Shadows

When the great hammer blow descended
it came suddenly, right out of the blue,
unexpected, out of a clear blue sky.
On the ground, moments before the blast,
it was a calm, sunny, Monday morning.

Those closest to the blast died instantly,
their bodies turned to crisp black charcoal.
Nearby birds burst into flames in mid-air,
and combustible materials like
paper, or skin, ignited instantly –
as far away as 6,000 feet from
the epicentre, or ground zero.
The white light acted as a huge flashbulb
burning the dark patterns of clothing on
skin and shadows of bodies onto walls.

Survivors outdoors close to the blast
described a literally blinding light,
combined with an enormous wave of heat.

*The city was hidden by that awful
cloud ... boiling up, mushrooming, terrible.*

Sixty years after that cataclysm
someone in power wrote the following:

*The war on terror involves enemies
hidden among us who hate our values,
who will use any weapons against us ...*

in the age of post-modern irony.

# Light and Shadow

The enlightened man looks
into the darkness and sees
at its heart the clear pure light:
The unenlightened man looks
into the light, sees only
the darkness in his own heart.

# Fire as Trophy

So many of our pagan poets
have stolen fire from the gods,
have raided heaven for their gifts
of words. Like Prometheus
they lie in deep darkness, chained
to the huge rock of their egos:
waiting for their vultures of guilt
to alight and torment them.

Out of their existential angst
they write dark verses of despair
on the void of their universe,
on their self-imposed loneliness,
their profound alienation
from the bright light of the Spirit.

# Roadmaps and Roadmaps: the Attraction of Opposites

Isn't it really very strange
how these roadmaps for peace
cause so much violence ---
perversely seem to lead to war?

Maybe it would be much better
if we designed a map for war:
perhaps then we would get some peace.

# Lebanon, July 2006: The U.N. Security Council Meets

As the bombs explode and the missiles fly
what's the number of this Resolution?
Is it 1697, did you say?
That's a long, long way from 242
(whatever you do, don't mention The War).

We must have an urgent ceasefire soon,
but not now, not immediately
(now is a moveable feast of slaughter).
But when all the bombs have exploded at
last and when all the missiles have flown,
then we might have an urgent ceasefire:
not now, not immediately ... but soon,
soon.

Orwell ... you didn't know the half of it.

# Lost in Samarra: One G.I.

You're lost in the rain of fire
and neither is it Easter-time
too: as the Iraqi death-toll
and the sun climbs higher,
you're looking in the Humvee
mirror, right down the avenue,
day-dreaming of going home –
negativity is written
all over you – and that's when
the IED just explodes all
around you, as you keep that
ill-fated appointment with death
in Samarra. And it's too late
now to ask the question why:
it's much too late to say goodbye.

# Blind Faith

Goya's art exploded
the myth of man as
a rational being –
opened Munch's troubled mind

and out came *The Scream*.

Yet, all our post-modern
cynics still call faith
blind: human reason
still their own strange faith –
even after all the
wars and holocausts

blind reason still blinds them.

# Moon shots and other shots

In mid-July, 1969,
U.S. astronauts landed on the moon:
In mid-August, 1969,
British soldiers landed on the hard streets
of Derry and Belfast. Those khaki-clad
young squaddies might just as well have landed
on the moon, for all the good they did.

# Pick a Bale of Cotton

The dispatches of General Sherman and
General Foster are as follows:
Savannah, Georgia, Dec. 22.

*To His Excellency, President Lincoln:*

I beg to present you as a Christmas gift,
the city of Savannah, with 150
heavy guns and plenty of ammunition,
and about 25,000 bales of cotton.

(Signed.)
W. T. Sherman, Maj. General.

# Shadow Land

Imperceptibly, it seems, we have moved
from the old Age of Anxiety
to the actual Age of Terror:
from the fear of the big atomic bomb
to the explosion of the small bomb,
from the balance of the superpowers
to the rise of the unknown powers.

Now we imagine the unseen spectre:
we have graduated from 'known unknowns'
to Donald Rumsfeld's 'unknown unknowns.'

We have moved into the Unknown Zone

# Chasing the Wind
*(after Thomas Merton)*

So our heritage
is useless labour,
the labour of science
without true wisdom:
toil piecing together
fragments that don't fit
pieces of the jigsaw,
the labour of action
without contemplation –
our faith in reason,
a reason without faith,
fleeing contemplation.

For all is vanity:
a chasing after wind.

*Pull down thy vanity.*

# In the midst of life ...
*(i.m. Robert Greacen d. 13-04-08)*

It's Springtime, April 2008:
colour has come back into the garden,
the grass is very green after showers;
under the pear tree there are golden flowers
and along the borders blue forget-me-nots,
with a couple of red tulips by the wall –
plant life returning in its yearly cycle.

In the midst of all this, there is news of death:
my friend, Robert Greacen, aged eighty-seven.
Also on this sunny, but cool, Spring day
they are burying Patrick Hillery,
former President, with due solemnity.

Looking out at the tree in my garden
I see the russet buds that soon will bloom
again into cherry pink and white blossom.
Another spring to savour: how many more?
A sad meditation. Enjoy this one.

Rest in peace, Robert, fellow Derryman
(this poet, too, can say *ich bin ein Derryman*)
fellow exile, poet and gentle man:
no longer an exile, you are home at last
not to 'wet and winds', but the lasting city.

# Getting One's Teeth Into Time
*(like John Ellis McTaggart)*

If one were wearing a philosopher's hat, then
one would have to doff it in honour of the great
John McTaggart Ellis McTaggart, deceased,
who once was an idea, a future thought,
before he became an actual presence;
and later, of course, an actual absence
receding forever into the passed past,
or should that not be the eternal future?

No matter. Hats off, then, metaphorically,
to the philosopher McTaggart McTaggart,
who became aware of Time's unreality
at some fixed, or unfixed, point in the circle.

# Written with a thin black pen
*(with a faded gold logo)*

Sitting alone in my own back garden, one fine spring day,
reading Ciarán Carson's latest opus, *For All We Know*:
The ambient noise of passing street traffic dies down
as reverberations from a plane, or helicopter,
ebb away. Then the sweet sound of a small singing bird
emerges, becomes distinct, enters into my ear,
as my consciousness focuses in on the beat of
the birdsong, wondering how many beats to the bar?
Find myself scanning the birdsong, just like a line of
poetry. It's a very complex structure, really –
seven syllables, as it were, followed by a six;
another six; six again; then a three, a trōchée;
was that last run an eight, or two fours? The trĩlls ring out
a subtle variation in the time, pitch and scale.
What class of bird is it? Always hopeless on singing birds:
apart from the blackbird, red robin and thrush, that is.
Rarely up early enough nowadays for the clear lark:
once upon a time used to hear its song quite often
rolling home like a shadow, after a very long night.
For all we know, it might even have been a nightingale.

# Quite Early One Morning

It really is very hard to beat
listening to deaf Beethoven's Fifth
within the Audio Department
of the Eye and Ear Hospital
on the still sweet Adelaide Road.

It's an entirely timely reminder
to update my audio technology:

sounds can change abruptly, nowadays.

# Title Not Needed

Give thanks for the wood pigeon,
the Dove of the Leaf
that cleared its ringed white throat,
sang unchanging song
trilled out its pure melody
on Adelaide Road one morning,
a road of verdant memory
a vista of urban greenery
after all the rain & so little shine
of this blessed year of Our Lord ...
Two thousand and eight,
the 2nd millennium.

# Sound Hieroglyphs in the Eye & Ear
*(for Ciaran Carson)*

Caught somewhere
between the eye
& ear sections
in the ENTHN
(Out-Patients)
Audiology
Department

I
listen
carefully
for the call

& watch
carefully
for the sign,
the
signifier ...

as staff
voices
rise
&

fall

calling out
names
first
&
last.

At night

all these
auditory
visionary
spaces
empty
ghostly

the sounds
of all
the names
& bodies
entirely
departed.

# David's Farewell
*(i.m. David Marcus d. 9/5/'09)*

There was something slightly incongruous
about the setting for your last farewell:
Mount Jerome's Victorian Chapel
with all those memorial tablets
on the walls for the relics of empire,
Major This, and Captain This-or-That.

The cemetery, though, was apt enough,
with all its Victorian decay –
near the entrance was the grave of Wilde
*père et mater*, missing its famous son
Oscar, lost forever to Père Lachaise:
Not far away were the bones of John Synge,
who 'lived with sunshine and the moon's delight',
'that enquiring man' wrote Willie Yeats;
here, too, the bones of Jack B. Yeats
the artist, visionary as the poet:
nearby were the remains of many friends –
James Plunkett, Ó Direáin and John Jordan –
you knew them all, David, read all their work.

After Mozart's piano sonata
16 and a Schubert Impromptu,
some verses from Ecclesiastes,
'To everything there is a season ...'
the curtain closed slowly on your coffin
and the congregation sang out *The Banks*,
'How oft do my thoughts in their fancy take flight ...'

Then, after eighty-four years, you were gone.

Outside, living friends murmured words of praise:
'He was Edwardian, a gentleman',
how you would have smiled at that, though pleased.

A pair of plumed horses, suitably black,
drew an empty hearse down the avenue,
leaving the shades of the dead to rest.

# Nine Mays Later
*(i.m. Michael Hartnett)*

Michael:
It is not my green garden
on this misty May morning
that makes me sad — all that
transfer of emotion
to the external seen
landscape is so yesterday,
all that Wordsworthian
personification —
no, this melancholy
is purely personal,
completely internal.

Yesterday a book arrived
with tributes and memories
compiled by your son, Niall —
*Notes From His Contemporaries:*
*Tribute to Michael Hartnett* —
reading it caused my sadness,
remembering distant days
in Leeson Street and the Green,
you declaiming your sweet verse
in that lilting voice of yours.

This May morning a fine mist
envelops my garden
so green, lush & full of life:
but the light is dull, sky grey,
as silence pervades this room
where I sit and remember.

Enough gloom: we need music
and a sean- nós singer,
a Limerick fiddler
and a pure tin-whistler
taking flight like a songbird,
dispelling all melancholy.

                      (14th May, 2009)

# Good Vibes

On my way to listen to
Paul Durcan read his verse at
The National Gallery,
who should I run into –
just down from the Shelbourne
on St. Stephen's Green – but
men in fluorescent jackets
bearing this great legend:

'National Vibration
Monitoring Service'

shades of :
'Danger: Men at Work'.

And if that doesn't shake your
tambourine, my friend, early
in the morning, then listen
to all those good vibrations.

(15-07-'09)

# Encountering the poet

It was a most peculiar dream,
Seamus, and you entered into it
when you appeared in my sitting-room,
where I was examining some books,
and asked me were there any there
that I wanted you to sign: there were
at least a half-a-dozen volumes
by S.H. The problem then arose
when I went over to retrieve them,
and somehow got stuck in the stacks,
my very body jammed into the shelves.

It was, I suppose, a writer's block.

You, to your credit, gave me a hand,
somehow extracted me from the shelves.
But when you set me down on my feet
was I the incoherent accident
who sat down to breakfast or, instead,
was I a poet's soul set free to fly?

I suppose only the new time will tell.

# The Season Turns

As I write out these abstract words
Miles Davis is playing a plangent
moody version of 'Summertime'
on my computer, a track from
*The Essential Miles Davis* album
that includes 'Round Midnight', 'Black Satin'
'Time after Time', and 'Bye Bye Blackbird' –
his cool trumpet sounds comfort my head.

Looking out at my quiet garden
I see for the first time this summer
a yellow leaf on the still green
cherry-blossom tree, autumn's harbinger:
the season's about to turn again –
though it seems summer has hardly begun.

# End of July

My eye is drawn to the one
yellow leaf in a tree of green.

The early morning sun lights up
that one leaf in its spotlight.

It glows golden in the morning:
at night it hides in the dark.

The year is turning, like the leaf.
My days are in the yellow leaf.

# Local Nightlight

Turning home into Clareville
from Larkfield, facing North,
the oval harvest moon glows –
shines brightly on Kenilworth –
newly-risen, pale yellow,
a pearl pendant, it hangs
low on the horizon,
as twilight's violet gleams.

# So slow, adagio

Some days now my life
appears to move so slowly
like the lone heron
high-wading in slow motion
through gently-running water
in the stream in Mount Argus.

The year's in the yellow leaf:
The sun's discus sinks lower.

# Gathering Rosebuds

The scripture of the poor is not secret
And neither is it a dream: it's hidden
Only from those who refuse to find it …
No more secret than a public garden.

# Nov. 2008, Dawson Street, Dublin

A large banner drapes the railings of
the Royal Irish Academy
proclaiming the legend 'Our War' –
referring to the First World War.

Well, it may be your war, RIA,
but I declare it never was mine.
And if they died for 'the secret
scripture of the poor', then they died in
vain, for that scripture is still 'secret'
after all these years, all those wars.

No: it was not my war —— none are.
When will the learned ever learn?

# The Cold at the Top of the World

On the North Ridge of Mount Everest,
in the area known as Death Zone,
under a shining cobalt-blue sky
a young mountaineer lay freezing
to death: in complete delirium
he had torn off his oxygen mask.
Up to 40 climbers passed him by
and left him to die alone in
the snow – some passed only feet away.
The young man's name was David Sharp:
the names of the others are unknown.
Seeking glory, they found infamy –
the cold hell of inhumanity.

May they be forgotten forever.

# By the Pool of Despond

There it is in the centre, hanging from the sky,
the secretive lodge of the King of Discord,
the large central hall of the twisted wizard.

Straight in front of it is no huge knotted elm
but a round metal tree, all its leaves Fools' Gold.
Here it was, they say, that all the vain dreams died ...

not a single acrostic leaf left unbroken.

Late at night waves of denizens can be seen
walking slowly backwards towards the temple's bars,
their glazed eyes set deep into their twisted heads.

All these well-dressed Cimmermen, who tried to see
too far ahead, now look behind themselves
and, retrograde, retreat into history.

Dream-like they pass on through the ivory gate,
lost in deep discourse, shapes shift into shadow,
as around them resounds an hypnotic beat ...

hidden in darkness, someone breaks off a bough.

Dense fog has obscured the descent through the arch
down to the river, which runs cold and dark
past the hall once free, now mired in debt ...

and way out to the sea where the moon will set.

# Early Flashback

The aroma of wooden pencils
freshly-pared, with the lead pointed,
brings me back so many, many years:
almost as far back as the days
of marla sticks, gaily coloured
before being rolled into a dun ball:
almost as far back as those lost days
of slabs of slates and bright coloured chalks –

and kindly schoolteachers now long gone.

# The Falcarragh Blues
*(In memory of my father, Hugh)*

Well, we didn't need a band to play
those long-lost Falcarragh blues:
the music kept playing in my head.

On my left the road led to the town,
on my right the long Line down
by the side of Ballyconnell Wood …

where a track led to the vanished home.

Across the road from the old stone school
we stood at the top of the graveyard field,
where all those ancestral bones lie hid …

and there we read the names and the dates
as in memory Hank Williams sang
about lost highways and lonesome blues.

For a moment the exile returned
to the street we once walked down
behind your cortege, down from the town

to lay you to rest long years ago.

How could I ever forget those blues:
How could I dance, without dancing shoes.

(23rd/24th May, 2010)

# Survival of the oddest

It's a question of natural selection:
Some wisps of grey hair from
the beard of Charles Darwin
have been discovered among
his papers, among his souvenirs
from his days on *The Beagle*.

Will these distinguished hairs
be venerated by all atheists?

# Christmas 2010

The sensuousness of snow:
my garden all marshmallow
smoothness, good enough to eat.
Five blackbirds sit brooding
on brilliant white branches,
the trees transfigured light –
meringue confectionery –
everything pristine, bright.

The birdbath wears a chef's hat
like a large coconut cream,
and our evergreen tree wears
a wedding dress for winter.

# Far Behind the Snow

The strange poignancy of snow in the city:
of awakening to blinds on my window
framed and bordered by startling light;
of the white marshmallow softness to the eye
of undisturbed snow cushioning my garden;
three new daffodils, their fragile yellow crowns
forlorn against the pure white under the bare
cherry-blossom tree still dreaming of April.

Why should unaccustomed precipitation
in February arouse sad emotion?
Is it that snow recalls Errigal for me,
its peak a white cone in winter –
or Muckish with brilliant mantle,
or Sliabh Sneachta, so aptly-named?

Snow's the real psychedelic experience:
watching floating flakes swirl and dance in the air.

# Code Name 'Geronimo'

Now the CIA imitates the Mafia –
'Osama bin Laden sleeps with the fishes'.

In Hollywood they are planning the movie:
Kurt Weill will score it, Coppola direct it

But who will play Osama of Arabia?
And why 'Geronimo', in the name of Allah?

# Digital Bytes ... The

Revolution will be televised:
first as a six-part series,
then later as a soap-opera;
with plenty of breaks for ads
and lots of product placements;
but it won't be free-to-air ...

The bidding for rights starts now.

# Movable Type
*(i.m.. Stevie Smith)*

o o f a r o u t o
o f a r o u t o o
f a r o u t o o f
a r o u t o o f a
r o u t o o f a r
o u t o o f a r o
u t o o f a r o u
t o o f a r o u t

too far out ....

# Almost Noon in Dallas

Oh, the yellow rose of Texas
is covered in fresh red blood:
it will never be yellow again.

Outside the Parkland Memorial
Hospital, shocked people stood
beside a large sign that read:

*Keep Right.*

Inside that hospital lay
the body of JFK.

At the Texas Theatre there sat
Lee Harvey Oswald watching
a movie called *War is Hell.*

Back in the darkened strip club
Jack 'Sparky' Ruby was oiling
his snub-nosed Colt Cobra 38.

HUGH McFADDEN is a poet, literary critic and freelance journalist. He was born in Derry, lived briefly there and in Donegal, before moving to Dublin. He has an M.A. degree in Modern History from University College Dublin (1968), with a thesis on 'AE (George Russell) and the Co-operative Movement in Ireland'. He was a Tutor in the History Department at U.C.D. in the 1960s and early '70s. Later, in the 1990s, he was a Tutor in Political Science at U.C.D., and a Lecturer in Journalism at the Dublin Institute of Technology (D.I.T.). For many years he was a staff journalist (News Sub-Editor) with *The Irish Press*: he was an Assistant Chief Sub-Editor there when the novelist John Banville was the paper's Chief Sub-Editor. He regularly reviewed books for the Press Group of papers, as well as for *Hibernia* magazine, *The Irish Independent*, *The Irish Times*, *The Sunday Tribune*, and *Books Ireland*.

He was a history researcher with The Irish Manuscripts Commission, and Editorial Assistant on *The Correspondence of Daniel O'Connell* (I.U.P., Blackwater Press 8vols.). He is the Executor of the Literary Estate of the writer John Jordan and has edited Jordan's *Collected Poems, Collected Stories, Selected Prose: Crystal Clear* (Lilliput Press, Dublin, 2006) and *Selected Poems* (Dedalus Press, Dublin, 2008). His own previous collections of poetry are: *Elegies and Epiphanies: Selected Poems* (Lagan Press, Belfast, 2005); *Pieces of Time* (Lapwing Publications, Belfast, 2004); and *Cities of Mirrors* (Beaver Row Press, Dublin, 1984).

Photograph: Glenda Cimino